Extraordinary Profits

from ordinary properties

About the author

Dolf de Roos began investing in real estate while still an undergraduate student. Despite gaining a doctorate in Electrical Engineering and owning an international technology company, most of his time is spent looking for, identifying, analysing and buying propitious properties. Dr de Roos is in demand throughout New Zealand, Australia and Asia for his compelling seminars on residential and commercial property investment. His first two books on property have been on the best-seller list simultaneously and for extended periods, and his columns are widely syndicated. He hosted the weekly two hour nationwide Property Show on Radio Liberty, and appears from time to time on television debates and interviews.

Extraordinary Profits
from ordinary properties

Dolf de Roos

Montage of house on front cover is a composite
taken from properties featured in this book

Distributed by:
Random House NZ Ltd
Private Bag 102950
North Shore Mail Centre
Auckland   New Zealand

Published by:
de Roos Associates Ltd
PO Box 14
Christchurch
New Zealand

First Printing : December 1997
Second Printing : September 2001
Third Printing : November 2002

Design and Layout by Creative Imaging Ltd

Printing by Team Print Ltd

© 1997 Dolf de Roos

ISBN   0-473-04866-3

Other books by the author

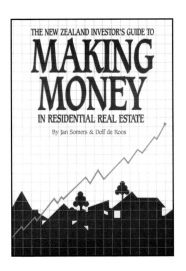

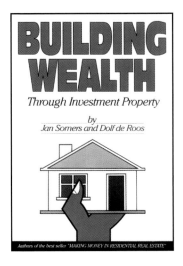

(Refer to last page for ordering details).

Courage does not mean having no fear.
Courage means acting despite your fear.

CONTENTS

extraordinary profits

1:   YIELDS AND RETURNS

Everyone likes to get a good return on investment, but few people ever measure returns accurately, let alone a develop a strategy for maximising them.

Instead, like the proverbial lamb to the slaughter, they often sell themselves short by considering only one narrow criterion when evaluating investments. Unfortunately, for most people this means looking at the yield.

When you are considering bank deposits, government bonds, or other forms of equity (cash) investments, then the yield is a crucial and relevant indicator of how your investment will fare. If you put up say $100,000 cash, then the yield tells you how much you will get back each year. Thus, a yield of 6% means that you will get $6,000 per annum from your investment. Now the true return will still depend on exactly when the $6,000 is paid. For instance, will it be paid in 12 equal monthly instalments of $500, or will it be paid quarterly, 6-monthly, or even annually? And will it be paid in arrears or in advance? These factors will slightly change the effective return on your money, but in essence you would receive around 6%.

This concept of yield is so ingrained in our minds, that when considering property investments, we all too readily accept the advice of some investment advisors, namely that since the yields on properties are typically in the 5% to 7% range, and since you can get a similar or better yield from other investments (which, the advisors are quick to point out, don't have all the hassles of property management), why bother with property?

This is of course a seductive argument. I know from having heard the stories of thousands of New Zealanders up and down the country during seminars, from my former weekly 2-hour talkback show, and from the countless letters that I receive each week, that many people are or have been put off because someone has pointed out that the yield is not as high as with other investments.

Indeed, I spend a lot of time dispelling the notion that property is not very good on account of the mediocre yields. The yield is only truly relevant when you put up all of the money required for the investment in cash. As we noted before, when you put up $100,000 cash to buy a bond, and you receive $6,000 per annum in return, the yield is a true indicator of how well you are doing.

However, when you buy a property, the yield is simply the ratio of rental income to purchase price. As such it is interesting, and even worthy of enquiry. But it certainly is not the basis on which you should decide whether or not to buy the property, let alone whether you should get into the property market.

The reason is obvious: while a property may cost $100,000 to buy, that does not mean that you have to put up $100,000 in cash. On the contrary, most people only put up between 10% and 30% in cash; the rest they borrow from a bank or other financial institution in the form of a mortgage. Many people even borrow the full amount required to buy the property.

What we are really interested in is not the yield, but what the Americans call the ROI or Return on Investment. In other words, you buy a property for $100,000, but arrange an $80,000 mortgage and only put up $20,000 in cash yourself. The real issue should not be what is the rent as a proportion of the purchase price (i.e. the yield), but what is the net return on your $20,000 cash input, after paying the mortgage interest, rates, insurances, and all other expenses, and after taking into consideration any other benefits such as tax-breaks associated with property investment.

Another useful measure of the performance of an investment property is to consider the cashflow sequence during a period of ownership. This will comprise the cash deposit, the net after-tax cash in or cash out each year, and the build up in equity, all the while taking the time value of money into account. This measure is called the Internal Rate of Return.

Now I have shown using the Property Investment Analysis software (see Appendix) that often properties with very modest yields may still have a surprisingly high Internal Rate of Return. Such analyses appeal to some investors, usually the "left-brain" or logical thinkers. However many "right-brain" or intuitive thinkers have trouble identifying with this notion. They prefer examples.

Often at my seminars, I give examples of properties I have bought, hoping that they will inspire others to seek out similar deals. Many people get fired up, but there are always those who say that with my knowledge and experience in property, such deals would be easy for me to find and act on, but almost impossible for the person on the street.

And that got me thinking. I can talk (and often do!) for hours on the merits of investing in property on account of the superlative cash flows, taxation advantages, growth rates, opportunities to increase values through improvements, and ability to buy at a price well below market value. However, why should I have to use persuasive arguments when there are literally thousands of actual real-life examples in every city or town in the country.

Ask most people on their retirement what their greatest asset is, and the vast majority will answer that it is their home. Not their share portfolio, or the car they bought for $60,000 back in 1982 when it was the latest of the latest, or their stamp collection, or their antiques. In nearly all cases it is their home, and you will hear the lament of many retirees who reflect and say: "If only we had bought two properties when we bought this one!"

Now my detractors will counter by saying things like: "No wonder, everyone needs a home to live in, but not everyone collects stamps or buys shares". Or they may say: "Sure, but when things get tough economically, people may be forced to sell their shares or collections, but few go to the extreme of selling their homes as they have to live somewhere". Of course, these arguments explain why property does not tend to have the volatility of other investments. Consequently, they are actually giving further reasons for a very real phenomenon, namely that property tends to be a stable investment that continues to go up in value with almost monotonous regularity.

Anyway, this got me thinking. Instead of showing my properties as examples of investments that have done well, why not ask fellow New Zealanders to share their experiences?

That was the whole idea behind this book.

At that stage I had no idea how the book would turn out. Indeed, initially I imagined that I would send out a letter asking for submissions comprising a photo and a brief summary on the property. I thought I would get a flood of bland data, and that I would compile it in an almost clinical manner.

However, when the submissions started to come in, I realised that what was being sent was not just bland information, but mini life-stories which encapsulated the essence of what I was trying to get across far better than clinical, tabulated data ever would. Amongst the submissions were tales of succeeding with little cash or cashflow, of overcoming perceived prejudices against age and gender, of learning along this path to prosperity, and overwhelmingly, of having lots of fun on the way.

I was inspired when I read these stories. And that's when I decided that rather than pick out the pertinent figures, I should include the text as written by the investors themselves. This book is largely a collection of success stories volunteered by New Zealanders just like you and me, doing things that you and I can also easily do.

Before any reviewer or critic attempts to suggest otherwise, this book is in no way an attempt to prove that property is a good investment. I have addressed that issue on numerous occasions in other books and articles, and on radio and TV shows. The contributors have not been selected at random – the fact that they comprise people who voluntarily contributed something indicates that they are probably biased when it comes to property. However, I cannot help but notice two things…

Firstly, nearly everyone can relate to the stories presented here, since nearly everyone has either experienced something similar, or has a friend or relative who has experienced something like this. I seriously doubt whether a book on successes from investing in bonds, equities, shares, futures, commodities, forests, exotic fruits, exotic animals, stamps, coins, antiques, precious metals or phone cards would ever get such a wide feeling of empathy.

Secondly, the scale of the profits relative to the cash inputs is truly astounding. With the exception of a few high-fliers, most people who can report profits from alternative investments are happy if they can turn a $5,000 investment into $8,000 in a few years. And for many New Zealanders, that is the order of magnitude of investment capital that they have available. Even if the capital available is much larger, doubling one's equity is considered phenomenal. However, when it comes to property, even though not much capital is required, the figures involved are suddenly in the hundreds of thousands, and a small percentage growth in property value results in a huge increase in equity.

Anyway, here follows a collection of submissions. They are not from hot-shot long-term property investors, but often from first-timers who are somewhat scared but excited all the same. They include stories from many parts of the country. They include the experiences of young couples, retirees finding themselves alone again, and Kiwis from the proverbial Struggle Street who have found initial success in the property market and are now dedicated converts.

Firstly, I will reproduce the letter I sent out inviting submissions. Then, by way of a lead-in, I will include some background on my family home in Dunedin from when I was a kid. At the time I never stopped to think of the financial implications of this property, but after it had been sold, I couldn't help but mull the figures over in my mind.

2: LETTER SENT TO MAILING LIST

de Roos Associates Ltd
PO Box 14
Christchurch

27th February 1997

Have your property appear in our new book
Subscribe to the New Zealand Landlord

Dear Fellow Property Investor,

The press is full of articles, commentaries, and opinions claiming that property is no longer a good investment. Sometimes the writers focus on a narrow variation of this theme ("residential properties will not increase much in the near future, so please invest in our commercial property fund"), but generally the message is: "Be careful, property may have been a great investment when inflation was bounding along at 18%, but with inflation capped at 2 or 3 percent per annum, you may be better off putting your money elsewhere". Well, you know what I (and history) have to say about that!

Everywhere I go, people are eager to relate stories about properties which they bought for prices that, looking back, seem like steals. Clearly, this applies to properties bought many years ago, but surprisingly to some observers, there are countless instances of recent acquisitions which also show phenomenal growth.

At my seminars I often give examples of my own acquisitions, and while they seldom fail to impress, sceptics think that such deals are beyond the scope, comfort zone and ability of the average property investor. Now that's where you come in...

Your success can be an inspiration for others. Let's get examples of properties that *you* have bought, and compile them into a book. What I imagine is one page per property, allowing room for a photo and some pertinent data. The data may include the location, purchase date and price, sale date and price (or, if not yet sold, current valuation), initial rentals, and final rentals. From these we will work out the number of years that the property was owned, and the annual compounding growth rate.

Then there will be some space for a brief narrative, where you may want to add information like "this house was truly the worst in the street, but after spending $12,000 it looked as good as all the neighbouring properties", or "initially it was under-rented at only $120 per week, but this immediately went up to $175 per week". Maybe you organised a good second mortgage, or got 100% financing. Let us know!

I envisage to feature about 100 properties, as I imagine that around 100 examples will give a good impression of the gains to be made, and how such gains can happen with ordinary, average properties, without managers, fund supervisors or other staff raking off their share. Of course it won't be definitive proof that property always is or will be a good deal. Indeed, our critics, and there will be critics who will fear that this publication may encourage people to go it alone and not give them their cut, will say that we have pre-selected the properties to show only those that show a good profit. But remember, the whole point of the book is to show that extraordinary returns can be had from ordinary properties.

Anyway, if your submission gets included in the book, we will send you two free copies of the publication. What we will want is a good sharp photo (black and white or colour - we will scan it and reduce it to black and white), and then all the information that you feel is relevant and interesting. No ten-page essays, please, but more than just the purchase and sale prices! Before and after photos would be good, but not necessary. Please tell us when (roughly) the photo was taken. We will collate the information, and send a "proof" of your submission (if selected) to you for verification. Then we can go to print.

Let's have a cut-off date for submissions of 31st March 1997. That should give most of you a month to chew this over, find, take or reprint a photograph, write some details, and send it all in. Naturally I will let you all know what progress we are having as we go along.

Finally, the excellent monthly newsletter *The Auckland Landlord* has gone nationwide. This publication is aimed at residential property investors, and now comes in three editions - the Northern Edition, the Central Edition and the Southern Edition. Called *The New Zealand Landlord*, it is full of timely tips, advice, comments, indicators, sales statistics, and trends, and features articles by economists, bankers, valuers and investors. I have agreed to write a monthly column for a while, and may offer to answer some of the many questions I receive through the New Zealand Landlord so that the answers may benefit more people than just the person who posed the question.

My advice is to subscribe, as you only need to get one good idea, and your $42 for a full year (11 issues) may be repaid many times over. Remember that *he who does not read has no advantage over he who cannot read.* You cannot put a value on good advice, and the subscription price is such that you would be a fool miss out. I have included an order form photocopied from their latest issue for you to use.

Hope to get your property submissions soon. Successful investing,

Yours sincerely,

Dolf de Roos

P.S. If you have a friend who would like to be on our mailing list, just send us their details.

1968

1978

extraordinary profits

3:   THE DE ROOS FAMILY HOME

16 City Road, Dunedin

Late in 1967, my family moved to Dunedin from Australia. After renting for a few months, we bought a house in City Road for £2,500 or $5,000. This house was about as plain as houses get – the sort of thing that kids draw at kindergarten – a rectangular box with a narrow door in the middle, a window on each side, and the obligatory chimney.

Now I concede that we did a few things to the house to titivate it, such as putting shutters on the windows, putting some dormer windows in the attic, swapping the narrow front door for a pair of so-called French doors, building a patio on the front, digging a sunk-in garden, and making numerous improvements inside the house. All these things can reasonably be expected to increase the value of the house over and above inflation.

However, the council also decided to widen the narrow City Road, and issued us (and all residents on our side of the street) with a notice telling us that we were going to lose around 12 feet from our front garden, or about a third of it. Although we got some monetary compensation, the loss of this land must have had a negative effect on the value of the property.

Nonetheless, by the time we sold 10 years later in 1978, we got $32,000 for the property, representing an annual compounding growth rate of over 20%.

The profit of $27,000 (excluding the council payment for annexing the land and the cost and time we spent titivating the place) was a capital gain and therefore tax-free. By contrast, my father's salary was income and therefore taxable.

In 1968, he was earning just on $2,000 per year, and by 1972 this had gone up to $5,000 per year – pretty average sorts of incomes for those times.

Taking into account the higher marginal tax rates prevailing at that time and applying them to his gross income during each year of the decade, then his after-tax income sequence accrued to a Future Value by the end of 1978 of less than $23,000.

In other words, my parents made more from owning this house for 10 years than they did from having my father work for 40 hours per week for 49 weeks of the year for 10 whole years.

I am not suggesting that my father shouldn't have worked – every family needs cashflow to pay for living expenses. However, the fruits of his 19,600 hours of work could obviously not be entirely invested.

By contrast, a spin off from the purchase of the house was that we also had a place to live.

What about the mortgage payments and the opportunity cost of the deposit? Well, in 1968 these roughly equated to the rent on a comparable property. By 1978 they were a small fraction of market rentals. And in the meantime, we had security of tenure (couldn't be kicked out) and could do to the place what we liked.

Looking back, I cannot help but wonder where my parents would have been if they had bought two (let alone 10) similar properties. The answer of course is obvious.

What probably put them off the idea (if they had thought of it in the first place) was an innate concern over having such a huge amount of debt. Whenever we look back at property prices 10 or more years ago, it is easy to see how static or falling debt slowly but surely gets swamped by increasing property values. At any time, however, it is difficult to accept that the same will continue in the future, and we baulk, unfortunately, at the thought of having total debts exceeding our net worth.

Anyway, it was around the late 1970s that I began to realise that ordinary properties offered returns on investment far in excess of what could generally be achieved from other investments. These extraordinary profits were achieved because (a) you could often buy a property for much less than its true market value (try that with shares!), (b) you only needed a small fraction of the purchase price in cash (the rest was willingly provided by mortgagees), (c) both the property and the rental income were indexed for inflation, (d) values were further fueled by demand through population pressures, and (e) there were superlative tax-advantages not available with most other investments.

Over the years I have told and written about many of my forays into the property market. On the following pages, many other New Zealanders tell their stories – in their own words – of how through luck or strategy they have made extraordinary profits from ordinary properties.

before

13.8.96 as bought

after

18.11.96 nearly finished

extraordinary profits

4: ORDINARY PROPERTIES: THE SUBMISSIONS

Acquisition:	**2 bedroom unit (77sqm) plus carport & private lawn**
Location:	**Papakura**
Purchase Date:	**August 1996**
Purchase Price:	**$56,000**
Government Valuation:	**$81,000 (1994)**
	$120,000 (1997)
Current Rental (per week):	**$220**
Current Market Valuation:	**$140,000 (May 1997)**

This was a mortgagee sale and was definitely the worst in the street. It had been occupied by street kids and everything that could be removed had been including the hot water cylinder and sink bench. Also 95 percent of the walls, roof and windows had been smashed or holed leaving basically just the framing. We borrowed the asking price plus $15,000 from the ANZ and got a three month holiday with a 'Yes Mortgage'. NZI gave us construction insurance. Other than a plumber, electrician and plasterer (for the lounge), we did all the work ourselves, every weekend and every night after work, over three months. The tenants moved in on 6 December 1996.

We borrowed against the unit itself but also have our own home mortgage with ANZ. Both ANZ and NZI were very supportive. A lot of hard work but in the end a very satisfying project.

Bryan & Elizabeth Rusden
Papakura

Acquisition:	2 bedroom leasehold property
Location:	Stewarts Gully, Canterbury
Purchase Date:	August 1995
Purchase Price:	$15,000
Government Valuation:	$48,000
Current Rental (per week):	$135
Current Market Valuation:	$60,000 + (May 1997)

Some time in August 1995 we arranged to meet with a friend and an agent to view a leasehold property in Riverlea Estates, Stewarts Gully, just outside Christchurch. We did this to encourage our friend to purchase a home. He never turned up and we were left to deal with the agent.

extraordinary profits

The agent informed us that he would present any offer to the vendor. We were reluctant to do this as we had no interest in the property, though after a chat in the kitchen we returned with an offer of $15,000 and advised the agent that this was a one-off offer and that we would not negotiate any counter-offer. We had made it subject to finance and L.I.M.'s plus the lease being acceptable to our lawyer. Our offer was accepted that day.

The Government Valuation at date of purchase was $48,000. The Government Valuation two months later was $53,000, we have had no independent valuation, although we would expect around $60,000 if we were to market it.

After purchase we had people literally queuing to rent the two bedroom property and some tempers flared though not ours. Rent for the first year was $125 per week and is now $135 per week.

The cost so far has been purchase and installation of electric range, installation of toilet and connection to high pressure water. In all, less than $1,000 as most of the preliminary work had been completed before purchase.

The predicted return was excellent and 100% financed along with another unit costing $80,000. This second property has recently been valued at $110,000. The combined rents total $295 per week. Loan of $95,000 at 9% fixed for 3 years (borderline negative gearing). Predicted compounding capital appreciation on $170,000 over the long term using information from *Making Money* (history) to be in excess of $400,000.

Really enjoyed your books and recently attended your seminar on inner city living in Christchurch. Also found your segment on Radio Liberty to be highly motivating.

Jim Russell
Edendale, Southland

extraordinary profits

Acquisition:	3 bedroom, large 1924 colonial house
Location:	Rimu Street, New Lynn, Auckland
Purchase Date:	November 1992
Purchase Price:	$95,000
Deposit:	$23,750
Bank Loan:	$72,455
Interest Rate:	8.2% to 9.95%
Rental (per week):	$210
Weekly Expenses:	$137.35 (including maintenance, renovations and interest but excluding principal repayments)
Sale Date:	November 1995
Sale Price:	$177,000

This was the original ad which led me to buying this property. $82,000 capital gain in exactly three years has got to be a good return on a $95,000 purchase and less than $24,000 cash input.

Marianne Buma
Auckland

before

after

extraordinary profits

Acquisition:	**3 bedroom bungalow on 1/4 acre section**
Location:	**Dublin Street Pukekohe**
Purchase Date:	**July 1994**
Purchase Price:	**$41,000**
Independent Valuation:	**$50,000**
Improvements:	**2 units built on subdivided rear of section**
Current Rental (per week):	**bungalow $185 and 2 units $230 each**
Further Improvements:	**$160,000**
Registered Valuation:	**$472,000 (September 1997)**

Purchase in July 1994 for $41,000, when asking price was $60,000. Property was in such a bad condition real estate agents wouldn't put signs on it. Was on market for 8 months and of the people taken there for viewing they took one look and discarded it as not worthwhile. We made $41,000 offer against wishes of real estate agent who didn't believe we had a chance at that level. Vendors did not even counter and accepted offer straight away.

Site was a 1/4 acre (1027m²) section on corner (absolutely ideal for subdivision). Existing house needed re-piling so was shifted to front of section to enable two units to be built on rear.

Original purchase $1,000 deposit and $40,000 loan taken against our equity. Another $30,000 borrowed to re-pile, re-roof, partially re-clad, re-plumb, re-wire. Fit new kitchen, alter floor plan from 3 bedroom with bathroom and laundry outside to 2 bedroom self contained, etc. A further $130,000 borrowed for two units on rear of site. All work done by owner (myself) – self-taught and learning fast builder.

Original valuation (independent) stated, "The dwelling has reached a stage where the cost of renovation would exceed the expected future market value." It stated value of site cleared at $50,000 minus $5,000 to remove existing dwelling, i.e. $45,000. Government Valuation was similar in that it gave a capital value $3,000 less than land valuation.

before

after

extraordinary profits

Lack of finances dictated that we rebuild the old house as opposed to demolish and build new at a cost of $70,000 approximately. Interesting to see that a dollar in/dollar out value on the old are comparable to the new houses built.

The old house took about six months to rebuild, which was longer than it took to build the two new units. Total cost of project over about 16 months was $201,000. Property has been subdivided into three titles.

Pukekohe has seen very good growth and the last valuation (12 March 1996) places bungalow value at $100,000 and two units at $125,000 each. Local real estate agents place current values of bungalow at $140,000 and two units at $155,000 each – total value of $450,000.

Original house was not getting any rent at all but two men were living there. Bungalow now gets $185 per week and units get $230 each.

This was not just the worst house in the street, it was easily the worst house in Pukekohe! Everyone told us we were mad – it's been great seeing them slowly change their minds.

Mark & Rhonda Jones
Pukekohe

View of the two units built on the rear of the section.

extraordinary profits

Acquisition:	2 x 2 bedroom flats plus single garage
Location:	Russell Terrace, Newtown, Wellington
Purchase Date:	June 1996
Purchase Price:	$105,000
Current Rental (per week):	$390
Current Valuation:	$150,000 (March 1997)

I purchased this run-down property at the age of 18 with a deposit of $10,000 (which took me two years to save). It is situated on Maori leasehold land (ground rent $252 per annum), which some people may stay away from, but from my investment point of view it's great. Instead of paying 9% interest on the $60,000 land value, I pay 4% of the land value which is fixed for 21 years (my current rental is based on a 1979 valuation!).

After purchasing the property, I borrowed $5,000 to paint the house and do repairs. Newtown then became Wellington's trendy new suburb, and a recent valuation concluded that its worth was now $150,000. I made $40,000 tax free in 6 months, more than what I would net in 2 years working at my current full-time job. I am now 19, and have sufficient equity to buy a second rental property.

What I have achieved shows that you don't need to be middle-aged or wealthy to start investing in property. It also helps banish the myth that buying leasehold land is a no-no. I would certainly buy further properties located on leasehold land.

Matthew Wright
Wellington

Acquisition:	2 x 2 bedroom flats
Location:	Felton Mathew Avenue, St Johns, Auckland
Purchase Date:	March 1991
Purchase Price:	$140,000
Current Market Valuation:	$295,000 (March 1997)

On 1 March 1991 I bought 2 x 2 bedroom flats, weatherboard with a tile roof, in St Johns, Auckland. These were on leasehold land but after checking with the Anglican Church Pension Fund prior to purchase I was told they were offering the freehold within 6 months. The purchase price was $100,000 and the land was offered to me 6 months later at $40,000. Total $140,000. The rents received at that time were $175 and $150 per week. The rates were $287 every 4 months.

My next move was to put them on separate titles, so that if in the future I need to sell one, I still have one left. At this stage these have been bought to keep, and I hope to keep them as my retirement fund.

I make sure that they are properly maintained and in between tenants, I always do painting, etc, to keep them in A1 condition. The lawns are mowed by a contractor, and gardens have been done by a gardener who has put weed-mat down to prevent the weeds.

In March 1997, when we had valuations done, and they were valued at $145,000 for the front flat and $150,000 for the back flat as this has a lockup garage.

Since I have bought this property, a University has been built nearby, and the location is excellent being 2.5 km from schools, 1 km from Glen Innes shops, 1 km from the Railway Station, and bus is adjacent to the property, which goes to Auckland City and Newmarket.

We have always purchased blocks of two flats – why …
1. If one is empty, the other is always tenanted.
2. Most people like to live in small blocks, no-one living above or below.
3. Always bought flats with separate titles.

I have been a follower of Dolf de Roos, and been to his seminars and read his books. By using his methods we now own four blocks of two – three blocks in one street (Felton Matthew Avenue, St Johns). I would strongly recommend property for a retirement fund.

Gloria Moller
Auckland

Acquisition:	3 bedroom brick and tile house
Location:	Appleby Crescent Burnside, Christchurch
Purchase Date:	September 1996
Purchase Price:	$116,000
Current Rental (per week):	$200
Current Market Valuation:	$150,000+ (March 1997)

My wife and I bought this house in September 1996 for $116,000. It is in Burnside and is not under the power lines – if you can see them in the photograph, the power lines are at the back of the houses on the opposite side of the street.

The reason for the house being so reasonably priced is that it was so run down, but I consider we got the "buy of the century". I don't have a "before" photograph but when we first went around to have a look at it I could see the potential.

The house is a 3 bedroom brick and tile on a 673m2 section, it has a double tin garage with a concrete driveway. It was a family home which had been left as an inheritance to one of the children and it literally hadn't had any paint or maintenance for the previous 30 years, all the inside was original – filthy, disgusting.

Also it hadn't been lived in for the last six years. It was impossible to drive up the driveway because it had flax growing completely across it. We got access to the house on confirmation for a painter to start on the job of completely redecorating it. This being five weeks before settlement so that the house would be ready to rent out without incurring the mortgage repayments.

The painter spent three days scrubbing the grime and fat off the kitchen ceiling and walls before he could even start anything else. I patched up a total of 25 holes in the gib-board where handles had gone through the walls and people had

extraordinary profits

obviously kicked. Being a builder I was able to do all the repairs myself, they turned out to be mostly minor repairs, i.e. installed a stainless steel bench, put a new secondhand vanity in and melteca on the walls of the bathroom, fixed up a couple of doors which were swinging the wrong way. The outside took a full day to waterblast from the roof and gutters, which were full of gunk to overflowing, to the drive, which was similarly blocked. The grass was fixed by hiring a commercial mower and the grounds cured by taking three trailer loads of rubbish to the dump.

To redecorate, new carpet, polished floors and new curtains, cost approximately $10,000 which we will be able to depreciate and claim against tax. With legal fees, etc, for around the $127,000 mark and a bit of hard work, which was also fun, we have what I consider an ideal maintenance-free rental property. If we were to sell it, a real estate agent has estimated it would sell in the current market in the $150's so on paper (not that we plan to sell) we have made $20,000-$25,000.

We have rented it out long-term and are getting $200 per week with potential to increase. Since this property we have also purchased another one, but not with such spectacular results. An interesting issue was we were advertising the house to rent while we were still doing it up and we were amazed that prospective tenants couldn't visualize the house in its finished state. The other thing I was scared about was, what if I couldn't rent it out, but these fears were soon allayed as the phone range red-hot and an endless stream of people wanted to drive by to view.

Jim Coote
Christchurch

extraordinary profits

Acquisition:	House + Granny Flat
Location:	Union Street
	New Brighton, Christchurch
Purchase Date:	1989
Purchase Price:	$82,000
Current Rental (per week):	$180 + $100
Current Market Valuation:	$140,000 (April 1997)

I never dreamed of having a mortgage, so when I purchased my first property in 1989 in New Brighton for $82,000 it had a sleepout on the back of the section, so I self-contained the sleepout making it a granny flat and lived in it, allowing the house to be rented out for $170 per week. I moved out in 1993 and rented granny flat for $100 per week and house for $180 per week. The property today has a valuation of $140,000.

I purchased my second property in 1993 in North Beach for $105,000, current valuation is $158,000. It has a granny flat rented for $100 per week, house rented for $190 per week.

I purchased my third property in October 1996 in the City (Bealey Avenue) at auction for $191,000, current valuation is $195,000. Again, double rental, I live upstairs and rent downstairs flat for $170 per week. I got 100% financing on this property.

As you can see I never dreamed of owning three properties, all double rentals, but the self-contained granny flats made that possible and pays all mortgages.

Johnny Moore
Christchurch

extraordinary profits

Acquisition:	House + Granny Flat
Location:	Pegasus Avenue,
	North Beach, Christchurch
Purchase Date:	1993
Purchase Price:	$105,000
Current Rental (per week):	$190 + $100
Current Market Valuation:	$158,000 (April 1997)

Acquisition:	House in 2 flats
Location:	Bealey Avenue,
	Central City, Christchurch
Purchase Date:	1996
Purchase Price:	$191,000
Current Rental (per week):	$170
Current Market Valuation:	$195,000 (March 1997)

from ordinary properties

extraordinary profits

Acquisition:	3 bedroom house
Location:	Subritzky Avenue, Mt Roskill, Auckland
Purchase Date:	November 1994
Purchase Price:	$123,000
Current Rental (per week):	$335
Registered Valuation:	$235,000 (December 1996)

First property purchased 8 November 1994 in Mt Roskill, Auckland with a purchase price of $123,000. The property was five years old and was previously rented at $235 per week. The house was handed over vacant by agreement and it was re-let for $315 per week. The house had curtains washed and walls scrubbed inside and out to present a fresh image. In December 1996 this house was valued by a registered valuer to act as security for further purchase of residential property at $235,000. A rent review for April 1997 placed the rent at $335 per week.

Second property, a brick and tile two bedroom house approximately 40 years old in Mt Roskill, Auckland, was purchased in February 1995 with a purchase price of $145,000. It was freshly renovated by a builder for resale with new carpets, new kitchen, new laundry and new paintwork inside and out. It was rented for $245 per week and in February 1997 a real estate agent estimated its selling price to be $205,000. A rent review in June 1996 placed the rent at $255 per week.

W. & P. Houston
Auckland

Acquisition:	2 bedroom house
Location:	White Swan Road, Mt Roskill, Auckland
Purchase Date:	February 1995
Purchase Price:	$145,000
Current Rental (per week):	$255
Current Market Valuation:	$205,000 (February 1997)

Acquisition:	3 bedroom house
Location:	Onekawa, Napier
Purchase Date:	December 1994
Purchase Price:	$91,000
Government Valuation:	
Current Rental (per week):	
Current Market Valuation:	$105,000

This 696m² property, situated in the suburb of Onekawa, Napier, is leasehold with the current lease being $900 per annum, expiring August 2008. The house was built in 1969, is weatherboard, has three bedrooms, sleepout and a double garage.

The property was purchased in December 1994 for $91,000 and was in tidy condition, enabling it to be rented out immediately on takeover. The property has a current market valuation of $105,000.

extraordinary profits

As can be seen by the PIA report, the property was essentially 100% financed, using my home as security for the mortgage.

I have since purchased two more similar rental properties with similar outlays and financing. Using PIA I have forecasted the three properties to give a total equity of $230,000 after a period of 10 years created by a combined initial outlay of only $10,000.

Murray Porter
Napier

PROPERTY INVESTMENT ANALYSIS SUMMARY

Assumptions		Projected Results Over	5 yrs	10 yrs
Property Value	$94,000	Property Value	$119,970	$153,116
Initial Outlay	$950	Equity	$28,226	$61,372
Rent per week	$180	After-Tax Return /yr	182.76%	141.43%
Cap. Growth Rate	5.00%		IF SOLD	
Inflation Rate	3.00%	Selling Costs	$5,099	$6,507
Interest Rate	8.75%	Equity	$23,128	$54,865
Marginal Tax Rate	33.00%	After-Tax Return /yr	179.45%	141.21%

COMPUTER PROJECTIONS OVER 5 YEARS

ASSUMPTIONS	1995	1 yr	2 yr	3 yr	4 yr	5 yr
Property Value	$94,000	98,700	103,635	108,817	114,258	119,970
Purchase Costs	$950					
Outlays	$950					
Loan	$91,744	91,744	91,744	91,744	91,744	91,744
Equity	$2,256	6,956	11,891	17,073	22,514	28,226
Capital Growth	5.00%	5.00%	5.00%	5.00%	5.00%	5.00%
Inflation Rate	3.00%	3.00%	3.00%	3.00%	3.00%	3.00%
GROSS RENT /wk /yr	$180	9,173	9,448	9,731	10,023	10,324
CASH DEDUCTIONS						
Loan Interest I/O	8.75%	8,028	8,028	8,028	8,028	8,028
Property Expenses	27.93%	2,614	2,692	2,773	2,856	2,942
PRE-TAX CASH FLOW	–$950	–1,469	–1,272	–1,069	–861	–646
NON-CASH DEDUCTIONS						
Deprec. – buildings	4.00%	2,632	2,527	2,426	2,329	2,235
Deprec. – chattels	$14,650	2,681	2,029	1,556	1,210	954
Loan Costs	$744	744				
TOTAL DEDUCTIONS	$0	16,698	15,275	14,782	14,422	14,159
AFTER-TAX CASH FLOW	–$950	1,015	651	597	591	620
RATE OF RETURN – IRR	182.76%					
Pre-Tax Equivalent	272.78%					

from ordinary properties

December 1994 (some windows still broken)

September 1996 (iron gates from dump)

Acquisition:	mortgagee sale house
Location:	Wanganui
Purchase Date:	September 1994
Purchase Price:	$30,000
Government Valuation:	$48,000 (1996)

Our property was bought in September 1994, in Wanganui, and about 200 metres from the Polytechnic. It was a mortgagee sale and the house itself was in a bad state of repair, having holes kicked in the gib-board, light fittings hanging loose, no doors inside, and some walls bombed with spray paint. It cost $30,000 and with some hard work, secondhand wallpaper and paint it was soon livable, because originally had been brought up to State Advances standards, with re-blocking, re-wiring and new guttering. The kauri doors were replaced having been found in the dump, along with a cast iron bed and bath. The bath was made into an outdoor one heated by a fire, which the students now centre their parties around.

The objective of buying this property was to get our daughter loan-free through the Computer Graphic Design course. The rent would provide an income for her to live on, and the additional expenditure should be regained when we sell, as the Government Valuation is now $48,000. I made the house freehold with my redundancy, and because I'm a Nurse I now have another job to help with any current shortfalls.

Hopefully there is another parent out there wanting to do the same thing, and the house still has heaps of potential for further development. It was also well fenced, with a locked side entrance, next to an Historic Villa with picturesque charm.

It's fun – students energize a house with their creativity. A glass-blower was there last year and he had all sorts of pieces placed around the garden and the bath, combined with driftwood. They are also nerve-wrecking too, untidy at times, but generally honest and neat people.

Louise Templar
Marton

extraordinary profits

Acquisition:	**2 bedroom home unit**
Location:	**Mayfield Road, Glenfield,**
	North Shore, Auckland
Purchase Date:	**March 1995**
Purchase Price:	**$120,500**
Current Rental (per week):	**$230**
Current Market Valuation:	**$180,000 (May 1997)**

Your property example book is a great idea and will be another effective way to assist anyone wanting to learn more about the business.

We are relatively new to the game and so far have only two properties as follows.

First property is a two bedroom home unit in Glenfield, North Shore, 1km from Glenfield Mall. Rear one of two. North end of block. Concrete block base, split stone, aluminium joinery, tile roof, PVC spouting. Single lockup garage plus parking for two cars. Large under house storage area. Fenced grounds, Situated down a ROW, close to Glenfield Mall, bus stop, etc. Purchased in March 1995 at purchase price of $120,500 through real estate agent. Government Valuation as at 1 September 1996: land value $58,000, improvements $107,000, capital value $165,000. Current market value circa $180,000 (based on recent sales in Glenfield area). Initial rental was $225 per week, current rental is $230 per week.

Unit is on a block base with garage under. Good views to north west. Was very tired when we bought so we repainted interior, new lino in bathroom and laundry. Not much cost but considerable time expended. Carpet needs replacement at around $2,000. This was our first investment property, we put in $30,000 cash and borrowed $90,000 on 25 year table mortgage from Trust Bank. We now realise we should have borrowed the full 100% (using home equity) but we are learning all the time.

extraordinary profits

Acquisition:	**2 bedroom home unit**
Location:	**Emirau Place, Glenfield,**
	North Shore, Auckland
Purchase Date:	**November 1995**
Purchase Price:	**$135,000**
Current Rental (per week):	**$230**
Current Market Valuation:	**$170,000 (May 1997)**

Second property is a two bedroom home unit in Glenfield, North Shore, less than 1km from Glenfield Mall. Rear one of two. North end of block. Concrete slab floor, concrete block construction with cedar facia at front, aluminium joinery, tile roof, PVC spouting. Small carport plus parking for one other car. Situated down a ROW in a cul de sac close to Glenfield Mall, bus stop, etc. Purchased in November 1995 at purchase price of $135,000 by private sale. Government Valuation as at 1 September 1996: land value $100,000, improvements $60,000, capital value $160,000. Current market value circa $170,000 (based on recent sales in Glenfield area). Initial rental was $220 per week, current rental is $230 per week.

Unit in secluded bush setting. Facing north to reserve with bush outlook. End of cul de sac, quiet and private. Very small unit with laundry in the bathroom. Carport is a tight squeeze. Not much storage. Had new paint and floor coverings when we purchased. Low maintenance. This was our second investment property, borrowed 100% against equity in our home and first investment property. Therefore loan was $135,000 on table mortgage over 25 years.

Gary & Catherine Dickinson
North Shore, Auckland

extraordinary profits

Acquisition:	**block of 3 flats**
	– 2 x 2 bedroom
	and 1 x 3 bedroom
Location:	**Princes Street,**
	Otahuhu, Auckland
Purchase Date:	**April 1995**
Purchase Price:	**$176,000**
Rental at Sale (per week):	**$165, $180 and $190**
	respectively
Sale Date:	**February 1996**
Sale Price:	**$253,000**

We purchased the property, a block of three flats, 2 x 2 bedroom and 1 x 3 bedroom, in Otahuhu, Auckland. Purchased in April 1995 for $176,000. The exterior was in sound condition, but the interior of the two 2-bedroom flats was very poor. Rents were increased immediately (within the context of the Act) from $145, $145 and $175, to $165, $165 and $190 per week. $20,000 was spent repainting the interior of all the flats, replacing the kitchen cabinetry in the two 2-bedroom flats, building a two-car concrete parking pad in the rear, putting a shower unit in one of the 2-bedroom flats, building a new garden in the front (with mowing strip), and fumigating all the flats. We did have some trouble with tenants, and used this as an opportunity of experiencing the tenancy tribunal twice. By the time the flats were sold (just got tired of the weekly hassles collecting rent) the rents were $165, $180 and $190. We sold the block privately after trying for several months using an agent, for $253,000 in February 1996. Net capital gain of $57,000 in 11 months on initial equity of $36,000 plus the $20,000 put in, is an annualised return of 111%.

H.B. Clow
Pukekohe

Acquisition:	3 bedroom house plus flat
Location:	Mt Smart Road, Onehunga, Auckland
Purchase Date:	October 1995
Purchase Price:	$178,000
Current Rental (per week):	3 bedroom $270
	1 bedroom $150
Registered Valuation:	$230,000 (March 1997)

extraordinary profits

We purchased the Onehunga property in October 1995 for $178,000. The property is a three bedroom house with single bedroom basement flat. The property has been rented at $270 for the three bedroom and $150 for the one bedroom. The property was in fair to average condition at the time. The previous owner had done a spec build on the rear half of the section, it was interesting to note that the previous owner had paid $178,000 for it also six months earlier, but had subdivided the back off of the section. This property has a March 1997 Registered Valuation of $230,000. We bought this property by borrowing 100% using our home as security through the ASB Bank. Interest rates were fixed for three years at 8.75%.

People are saying that you cannot purchase a property in Auckland at the moment that is positively geared, but it is possible. Like all renters in the bottom end of the market, all have positives and negatives. And this property is one which from a business point of view is okay.

Acquisition:	3 bedroom flat plus flat
Location:	Jane Cowie Avenue, Otahuhu, Auckland
Purchase Date:	March 1997
Purchase Price:	$189,000
Current Rental (per week):	3 bedroom $280
	1 bedroom $175
Current Market Valuation:	$230,000

This Otahuhu property was purchased in March 1997. The property is a three bedroom flat and a one bedroom flat, attached, and brick and tile. The property was presented in good condition as it was just done up by an entrepreneur. The three bedroom has a large carport and a lockup garage (which I intend to use to convert the one bedroom into a two bedroom). The one bedroom has an enclosed garage but with no door. Now the disadvantage of this property is that it is leasehold and it cost a whopping $189,000. But it's a good earner bringing in $280 plus $175 per week.

I hope this is the sort of thing that you are after. We have five other rentals which show better returns than these but were purchased in 1992-1993 when it was hard to go wrong.

I have read your books and heard you speak on several occasions. You know the message is simple, but I still get a real buzz out of hearing it.

Garth & Cheryl Cutfield
Auckland

Acquisition:	**4 flats – 1 x 1 bedroom, 2 x 2 bedroom, 1 x 4 bedrooms upstairs on land area of 1384m²**
Location:	**Ranfurly Street, Christchurch**
Purchase Date:	**June 1991**
Purchase Price:	**$206,000**
Rental at Sale (per week):	**$595**
Sale Date:	**June 1996**
Sale Price:	**$340,000**

At first, we were going to purchase the property in partnership with my wife's parents. We got a first valuation prior to purchase of $213,000. The first accepted offer was $210,000. We decided after the purchase to get a second valuation, this one was $195,000 and not too positive. Also a junior valuer I knew told me that he knew the property very well having valued it two years earlier, his valuation at the time was

$155,000 and he told me that anything above $175,000 would be too much as it needed much work, and had changed hands three times in five years.

Fearing to take my in-laws down with us, I asked them to leave the partnership. We then made a new offer of $204,000 … as it was all we could afford on our own. They countered at $206,000 three days later, I finally accepted reluctantly as my wife and I had agreed that our last offer was our highest.

It took me nine months (nearly full time as I was a house father at the time, using creche and granny to free my hands … working weekends as well … which brought its share of friction with one or two tenants) to bring it to standard, painting much of the inside, all of the outside, repairing what needed doing. The rent could not be raised as it was reasonably high at the time of purchase, which was another disadvantage to buying it, as I was well aware at the time. We managed it as if we were to keep it for 20 years, new carpet in two flats, new roof, so that at the time of sale it was a breeze to manage.

We heard of the neighbouring property going to developers, we were looking at buying a commercial property, and realising that we would need liquidity to do so, we offered it to them. Our latest valuation was four months old at $325,000. I had previously asked our real estate agent if this valuation was real … he replied to my surprise that it was a bit conservative, and should he list it, he would start at $350,000 aiming at $330,000 in our hand. With this in mind, we set the price with our purchasers. At the time of sale, we owed $210,000 on it. The property was demolished in November 1996, the land is now the entrance to the Fernwood Village project, as well as two of the projected properties. Most of the garden, which comprises some mature plants like a 60 year old rhododendron will be preserved and integrated to the new project.

Felix Forgues & Claire Wilson
Woodend

before

after

extraordinary profits

Acquisition:	2 bedroom unit
Location:	Papatoetoe, Auckland
Purchase Date:	December 1986
Purchase Price:	$54,000
Registered Valuation:	$90,000 (January 1990)
	$129,000 (March 1996)
Current Rental (per week):	$175
Current Market Valuation:	$140,000-$145,000 (May 1997)

A 2-bedroom unit, brick/cedar and tile, located in a good part of Papatoetoe, Auckland (in block of four) was purchased in December 1986 for $54,000. Initial rent was $130 per week, currently under-rented at $175 (market rent $200 to $220), however, excellent tenant of four years with no intention of leaving.

Property was placed on the market mid-1985 by the Public Trust, but due to legal problems with probate, was later withdrawn off the market. In September 1986 I heard property was to be placed back on the market, possibly at the previous years asking price. Subsequently, I made an offer at the asking price, realising it was being under-valued and hoping such an offer would have a fairly good chance of being accepted by the Public Trust. It took some three months of fighting its way through bureaucracy, but was finally accepted.

The property had been vacant for some 18 months and needless to say, was in need of a total "Birthday". The rear lawns were waist high and exterior in need of a good waterblast and paint. The interior needed paint and paper, and a shower fitted over the bath.

At age 20 and full of excitement and enthusiasm at my first property purchase, the redecoration was no great hardship, and nothing a few late nights after work and weekends wouldn't fix.

Nigel Smith
Auckland

Acquisition:	**3 bedroom townhouse**
Location:	**Montana Avenue, Murrays Bay,**
	North Shore City, Auckland
Purchase Date:	**December 1993**
Purchase Price:	**$180,000**
Government Valuation:	**$275,000 (1996)**
Current Rental (per week):	**$280**

Purchased 3 bedroom townhouse with one and half bathrooms on cross lease site in Murrays Bay, North Shore City in December 1993 for purchase price of $180,000. Rent received $260 per week first two years, $280 per week remaining 18 months.

The house is close to sought after Primary, Intermediate and Secondary Schools (Rangitoto College) and is walking distance to Murrays Bay Beach.

When purchased, the house was the only house on the left hand side of the road – an orphan, however as suitable land close to beach and schools became scarce and property value increased, the land either side has now been purchased and developed. The house is no longer in isolation and its value has rapidly increased.

Since purchase, the property has been occupied by one tenant. Rental properties are sought after in this area because of schools and beach. The tenant signed up before settlement date having only looked at it from the street.

R.G. Donohue & S.J. Miles
Auckland

Acquisition:	block of 3 flats – 2 x 1 bedroom and 1 x two bedroom
Location:	Thames
Purchase Date:	October 1991
Purchase Price:	$68,000
Government Valuation:	$128,000 (October 1996)
Current Rental (per week):	2 x 1 bedroom $130 each 2 bedroom $160
Registered Valuation:	$128,000 (October 1996)

In October 1991, after years of telling ourselves we should be buying rental properties, we purchased our first block of three flats on 328 square metres of land for $68,000. Mortgaged 100% against our own home.

Constructed originally as a miners cottage, the building was converted into a school takeaways shop about 1930, and closed in the mid-1950's. The various lean-toos around the main building were used to create the three flats which are legal and remain under "existing use rights". The land is zoned commercial town centre and located in central Thames, half a block from the main shopping street.

The rents provided an excellent cashflow for first time property investors. Two by one bedroom at $80 each per week and one by two bedroom at $90 per week. The previous owners (an estate) had allowed continual neglect by tenants and left years of damage and dirt unattended. We could see past that. As existing tenants moved on, we repaired and redecorated the flats back to a more habitable condition. This cost about $20,000.

As at 1 October 1996 we have a registered valuation of $128,000 and rent returns of $130 per week for the single bedrooms and the double at $160. This year will involve us spending about $10,000 repairing and maintaining the weatherboard exterior. After this we expect the valuation to be around $160,000.

When we talk with friends and relatives so many of them seem to regard investment in "bricks and mortar" as boring. Mind you, our flats were made more out of paint, dry rot and borer when we initially bought them. However, as our first investment, other than our family home, they have had great returns, been a very safe investment, hardly ever empty because of their close proximity to the town centre (we look at rent coming in for 52 weeks of the year, very little down time), and have been invaluable as a learning tool in property investment. Something we have cut our teeth on, so to speak.

For our personal development and as a learning tool for our family, it has been wonderful. You see we were not wealthy people. We were also not overly well educated, and had the handicap of basically working class background. I say "handicap" as our initial battle in looking at investing was probably more in the mind than to do with finances. We didn't really have friends or family who invested, so the culture of it all was really foreign to us. We definitely stepped out of our comfort zone. The children were then 6 and 4 years old. Job security was uncertain. What has changed in that time is, the children and us are older, job security is still uncertain, but since those early beginnings of 1991, we have generated enough income with our investments, to effectively replace one income, if we were to lose jobs. This extra income we are now able to enjoy, in leisure activities (the first major bonus we had, we took the kids to Disneyland), or spend on necessities in life. I used to wonder where we would ever find the money for our eldest daughters orthodontic treatment, let alone being able to fund their tertiary education.

For the children, the most valuable lesson they are learning, is one of investing for financial independence. They're able to tot up the figures on a calculator, just about as fast as the best of us. The kids have developed great social skills. They competently handle phone calls from tenants, or prospective tenants. They will talk with people from a wide variety of backgrounds, and recognise that other people have their opinions, philosophy on life, and are able to weigh it all up and so we hope enable them to make wise choices in their lives.

Megan & Kevin McCarthy
Thames

from ordinary properties

Acquisition:	3 bedroom unit
Location:	Panama Road
	Mt Wellington, Auckland
Purchase Date:	September 1995
Purchase Price:	$115,000
Current Rental (per week):	$250
Current Market Valuation:	$150,000

I am a solo parent and I knew I could do it if I had the information. I went to one of your seminars and read your book *"The New Zealand Investors Guide to Making Money in Residential Real Estate"* about three times and saw Barry Scott from New Zealand Realties in Auckland. He put all of my relevant information into his computer with your software and told me I could invest in something up to $120,000.

In September 1995 I found a three bedroom, split-stone, aluminium joinery and tile roof unit in Mt Wellington going for $115,000, it was in a block of six – three owner-occupied and three let out. It was clean and tidy, and was in an area which was improving. I decided to take it.

I had equity in my own home and was able to get 100% finance for the unit. I managed to get an interest only 9% mortgage fixed for a year. I put the unit in the hands of a letting agency who have been really good. We started out getting $220, and when those tenants left, we put the rent up to $250 per week. In one and half years it was empty for two weeks and is now valued at $150,000.

I'm now working hard and looking for another small property to invest in. My superannuation is under way.

Wendy Doust
Auckland

extraordinary profits

Acquisition:	**townhouse**
Location:	**Riccarton, Christchurch**
Purchase Date:	**January 1995**
Purchase Price:	**$140,000**
Registered Valuation:	**$140,000 (October 1994)**
	$155,000 (August 1995)
	$175,000 (November 1995)
Rental at Sale (per week):	**$275**
Sale Date:	**January 1997**
Sale Price:	**$194,000**

The first property (Unit 2) was purchased off the plans along with Unit 1 (which we still own – purchased for $145,000, present registered valuation $198,000), and Unit 3 (purchased for $150,000 and sold one week after taking ownership for $166,000).

The area at purchase time was largely a Student rental area, with a number of rundown properties. It was easy to see that this area was soon to change due to the close proximity of Hagley Park, Riccarton Mall, and the city. With the pending changes, property values would increase, rents would increase, and the students would eventually move to make way for the "inner city living" breed of people.

We had an abundance of people wanting to rent the properties, and I put this down to two things. As Bob Jones would say – Location, Location, Location, and this goes for renting also. Own properties in desirable areas, and you should not have too much problem finding a suitable tenant – as long as you are not too greedy with what rent you want of course, and are asking the market price!

The other area is the quality of your property. People will treat a rough property accordingly, and treat a well-maintained property as such. This has been my experience over the last ten years.

Grant Cartwright
Christchurch

extraordinary profits

Acquisition:	**2 bedroom unit**
Location:	**Antigua Street, Christchurch**
Purchase Date:	**July 1995**
Purchase Price:	**$97,500**
Rental at Sale (per week):	**$180**
Sale Date:	**April 1997**
Sale Price:	**$121,000**

In July of 1995 I decided to invest what was left of my divorce settlement into something that should make a profit for me and also give me some income. I decided to buy a property as I had once owned an investment property and found it a good sound investment.

I bought Flat 4 at 88 Antigua Street in Christchurch. They were asking $104,000 but I bargained them down to $97,500. When I took it over it looked a bit run down so I got a painting contractor in and he quoted $800.00 to plaster some walls and completely paint the unit. After this was finished I cleaned up the grounds around the flat and rented it out at $160.00 a week, which more than covered my mortgage payments.

I had put in $27,500 cash and borrowed $74,500 at a fixed rate of 9.5% for one year, interest only. I was only paying back $150 a week, leaving me $10 a week ahead. After three months the tenants decided to leave and it was close to Christmas. So I moved into the flat for three months and paid the mortgage interest myself. I realised that this is not the way to make money, so I put it back on the rental market at $180.00 a week on a one year contract (plus the tenants had to pay the security system rental of $30 a month). I got a Korean couple who were very keen to rent it and they were great for the first 9 months. Then they left. I decided to sell the property and it was sold within one week of going on the market for a total of $121,000. Not a bad profit for my brief period of ownership.

Matt Matthews
Christchurch

extraordinary profits

Acquisition:	**1 x 3 & 3 x 2 bedroom flats**
Location:	**Carlton Mill Road,**
	Christchurch
Purchase Date:	**1993**
Purchase Price:	**$302,500**
Current Rental (per week):	**$655**

When we first saw this property for sale in 1993 the asking price was $315,000. We offered way below $300,000, but eventually agreed to a price of $302,500. This seemed somewhat expensive for a 4-flat complex, but then again the location (Carlton Mill Rd in Christchurch) is very good as it is close to town, close to the river, and almost next to Hagley Park.

The flats comprise one 3-bedroom unit and three 2-bedroom units. The initial rent on the 3-bedroom unit was $155 per week. Now, four years later, it is $180 per week, although we're sure we could get between $200 and $210. We're a bit soft because the tenant has been there for the last three years.

Three years is nothing compared with one of the other tenants, however: she's been there for 29 years, which is why her rent is still at $150 per week. We cannot imagine changing it in the near future, either.

When the bank manager found out that we were buying this property with very little cash (we borrowed nearly everything) he penalised us 1% on the interest rate, saying that he would drop it ½% once we put in $32,000 of equity.

So, in 1994 we had the property revalued, and the valuation came in at more than $32,000 above what we had paid for it. We went back to the bank, pointing out how we now had more than $32,000 equity in it, and true to his word he dropped the interest rate ½%.

We haven't had it valued since 1994, but feel that with the rent roll, the increase in value, and the tax advantages, it has been a very good investment, especially when you consider that we hardly put any cash into it ourselves.

Harvey & Katrina Brehaut
Christchurch

Acquisition:	**suburban villa**
Location:	**Alpha Avenue,**
	Christchurch
Purchase Date:	**1973**
Purchase Price:	**$13,750**
Sale Date:	**1975**
Sale Price:	**$21,000**
Current Asking Price:	**$295,000 (October 1997)**

My husband and I bought this property from my sister back in 1973. Since it was a transaction between friendly family members, we didn't want either party to be disadvantaged, so we got the property valued. The valuation came in at $13,750 and that was therefore the price that we paid.

Initially it was our intention to live in the property, but through various circumstances that never happened. For two years we had the place rented out – I forget the exact rental figure, but it was around $20 per week. Of course this was not a bad return, considering that there was nothing that needed doing to the property.

However, two years later, realising that it wasn't fulfilling our initial intention of being the family home, we decided to sell. By 1975 the market had shifted considerably, and we sold it for $21,000. This represented a capital gain of more than 50% in just two years.

Needless to say we thought we had done pretty well. And we continued to think so until a couple weekends ago, because I happened to see the very same house advertised in the Christchurch Press. In the 22 years since we got our $21,000, the asking price has gone up to $319,000. Last week they were advertising for "offers over $295,000". Even using the latter figure, when you work it out, that represents a compounding capital growth rate of 12.8% per annum from the $21,000 we got in 1975, or 13.6% from the $13,750 we paid in 1973. And if we had kept it, not only would we have got the extra capital gain, but we would also have had 22 extra years of receiving increasing rents and tax breaks.

We do not lament the fact that we sold. We lament the fact that we sold and didn't buy a second property.

Mrs Cartwright
Christchurch

extraordinary profits

Acquisition:	**character home in 2 flats**
Location:	**Te Aroha Street, Hamilton**
Purchase Date:	**December 1991**
Purchase Price:	**$69,000**
Rental at Sale (per week):	**$325**
Sale Date:	**December 1996**
Sale Price:	**$135,000**

My example of a property in Hamilton is a classic example of how to buy a property with little or no money, renovate, rent and then realise a considerable capital gain. The property sold in December 1996 for $135,000, purchased in December 1991 for $69,000.

It was a large character home divided into two flats, extremely run down and messy. The two flats were realising $90 for one flat and $110 for the other. I set about renovating it and turned it into a five bedroom house at a cost of $12,000. It was then re-let out at $65.00 per room or $325 for the house.

C.L. Fawcett
Hamilton

Acquisition:	4 bedroom villa
Location:	Burke Street, Christchurch
Purchase Date:	1985
Purchase Price:	$43,500
Sale Date:	1987
Sale Price:	$64,800

Back in the mid 1980s, my brother and I bought a 4-bedroom villa dating from around 1908 in a residential street not far from the centre of Christchurch. We managed to buy it with very little cash input. It was a bit run down and in need of some attention such as painting and some new flooring, which we did ourselves. In total we spent around $6,000 doing it up.

I had always remained friends with my first girlfriend, Liz and her brother Andrew Miller. Andrew, whom I'd known since he was 8, was at that stage looking for a flat, and presto! the house was rented out. Andrew took on three flatmates, and after a while started dating one of them, Therese. Today they are married and have two children. We all still see each other every now and then and are friends to this day.

The villa was rented out at a market rent of $180 per week, which represented a healthy yield of around 20%.

Anyway, we paid $43,500 for it in 1985, but less than 18 months later were offered $64,800. Even though it had been our intention to rent it out long term, the capital growth was very tempting, and we accepted the offer, thinking we had done very well.

Looking back, it may have been better to hang on to it, as today it would be worth at least $135,000. The moral of the story of course is to never sell!

Peter & Ben Evans
Christchurch

Original cottage

Acquisition: **central city villa**
Location: **Chester Street East,**
                           Christchurch
Purchase Date: **1976**
Purchase Price: **$1,950**

Chester St East used to be a dump! That's telling it like it is: rat-hole flats with overgrown vacant sections. However, as the adage states: all bad things must come to an end! Chester St East has become prime real estate. I purchased a little cottage, typically constructed from plans imported from England with the living areas devoid of sun.

The purchase was made in 1976 for $1,950 which still represented a hefty mortgage in those days.

I lived there until the early eighties, when I was bequeathed some money. After much deliberation on the possible permutations and combinations on what I could do, I decided to subdivide, and built a most attractive house on the rear section. Now I have heard some horrific stories about buildings going over budget and having ongoing battles with the City Council. However, it would appear that if you treat the bureaucrats with less contempt than they deserve, they can be pleasantly co-operative.

Avoiding being a typically aggressive Kiwi can help considerably. The builder was helpful as well in keeping the costs within budget. I simply said to the builder and subcontractors as the construction progressed: "Go over budget and there is just no more money", that simple!

The existing older property was rented out for $180.00 per week. The real estate agents said start at $150, but I took a punt and so far, some minor hiccups notwithstanding, the tenants have been good.

House built on rear of section

extraordinary profits

Collectively the properties have a value of $375,000 today. With the considerable improvements that have taken place in the street, in the form of flats and townhouses sprouting with crazy abandon, values look set to increase even more. I think it boils down to the old saying: "all things come to he who waits".

Several times I tried unsuccessfully to sell up, but I was between a rock and a hard place. The house had little value, the land had little more, and the street at the time was pretty grotty.

However eventually, as history proves, growing populations in the cities create demand. As more accommodation was needed, old houses were demolished and new flats and apartments replaced them. My property simply came along for the ride by going up in value.

The future: to demolish the old cottage and rebuild a free-standing house, thus adding value to the land. I once heard that your property should double every decade. Well, given my initial outlay, I feel that the increase in capital value has been quite good.

Alistair Paterson
Christchurch

Acquisition: 3 bedroom property
Location: West Auckland
Purchase Date: July 1985
Purchase Price: $110,000
Current Rental (per week): $230
Current Market Valuation: $160,000 (March 1997)

Here are some details with regard to a three bedroom investment property that we bought in West Auckland.

The property was purchased in July 1995 for $110,000. As you will note in the enclosed colour photograph, the property was in good order, and apart from spending approximately $350 half share on replacing a much needed board fence (between the neighbours), this was the only money that needed to be spent on the property. Initially it was rented at $200 per week, and as at January 1997, when we had an offer to sell the property for $160,000, the rent (at that point) was $230 and subject to a further immediate market review, which would possibly have taken it up to around $260 per week.

Initially the property was valued at $103,000 and was one of two units. We were initially going to purchase the second unit, but were unable to negotiate a satisfactory price. We observed that the owner of this unit was devaluing his property, as he had a collection of very old cars parked upon it, and it was also known that he was having marital difficulties. In light of this, we thought there was a good opportunity to buy this unit at a cheaper price, however, decided in the event to turn it down and realise our capital gain whilst we could. This has now been applied to our new property.

We bought a further property – a three bedroom standard weatherboard home plus detached modern one bedroom unit on the same grounds – in Henderson, in May 1997 for $280,000. These are rented for a total of $460 per week and already my property manager advises that the tenant of the larger wishes to purchase the lot, once her marriage settlement is due about January next, for around $330,000-$340,000. This is on a supposedly flat Auckland market! Of course, the proof is in the reality, but it looks promising.

Brian Cranstone-Hunt
Auckland

from ordinary properties

extraordinary profits

To finish off with, here is a letter I received, not in response to my mail-out seeking submissions, but totally out of the blue and unsolicited. It speaks for itself.

March 1997

Dear Dolf,

Interesting point – the lambs I sold before Christmas were worth $20 for 12 kg, exactly the same price as in 1976!

With all that inflation they've stayed the same! Meanwhile the local houses are five times the price!

With no inflation over the next 20 years, what will the price of lambs do?

Thoughts like this make me pleased I read your book and bought a few houses.

We could never have bought this place without our residential rental profits. I'm sure it'll rise nicely in value too.

Lex & Angela Severinsen
Takapau

Appendix:
Investment Analysis by Computer

As discussed in Chapter 1, yield on its own is not a good indicator of the investment potential of a property, as the yield of an investment property is simply the ratio of rental income to purchase price. As such it is of little value in determining what the return will be on your invested capital.

Working out the rate of return on any investment is basically a matter of analysing what you put in compared to what you get back at the end. In the very simple case of cash invested in a bank, what you put in are the deposits and what you get back at the end will be the sum of these deposits plus the interest accrued each year, less the tax you pay. The rate of return is effectively the interest rate that the bank offers minus the tax you would have to pay at your marginal rate.

With property investment, the rate of return is still calculated from what you put in compared to what you get back. However, the equations are much more complicated than those for cash in a bank. For a property where you have a large initial deposit, what you get back would be the positive annual after-tax cash flows plus equity build-up in the property. Where you have little or no initial cash deposit, the annual after-tax cash flows (net rent plus tax refund minus interest) would be negative. In this case, what you put in would be your annual contributions to cover this deficit, while what you get back would simply be the equity build up. The real rate of return is effectively the "interest rate" that you would have to receive on these after-tax contributions to attain the equity at the end. This percentage is termed the Internal Rate of Return (IRR).

To estimate the rate of return on a property in advance, you must make some assumptions and projections for all the factors that determine your after-tax costs (these will change each year) and the growth in value of the property. The IRR is then calculated by trial and error such that the sum of your annual "deposits" plus the "interest" each year is equal to the equity at the end.

For instance, assume you have bought a property with a certain cash deposit, and that the annual after-tax cash flows are positive (total income exceeds outgoings during the year). Then the Internal Rate of Return is simply the return or interest rate that a bank would have to offer you, such that if you had given the bank the cash deposit, the bank could afford to give you the same annual after-tax payments, and at the end of the period being considered also pay you the equity that has built up in the interim.

The concept is really very simply. However, although it is possible to calculate the internal rate of return manually, the number of factors that need to be considered, together with the tedium of using a trial and error method, make the use of a computer program very attractive.

We have developed a computer program designed specifically to determine whether a prospective property investment is a good proposition. Called Property Investment Analysis, the program takes account of all the factors that determine the performance of an investment property.

PIA is extremely useful when looking at a number of potential investment properties, and trying to decide which one to proceed with. It is often difficult to compare all the factors that make each property unique. For instance, is a $200,000 property with a rental of $360 per week and a capital improvements value of $120,000 a better investment than a property costing $320,000 with a rental of only $500 per week (a lower yield) but with a capital improvements value of $250,000 (i.e. greater depreciation)? So far we have only introduced one factor over and above the purchase price and rent, and already it gets confusing.

The benefit of calculating the IRR is that you can directly compare two properties with wildly different factors such as purchase prices, rentals, depreciations, costs, and interest rates.

Often, PIA will identify a property with a modest yield as being a good investment with a relatively high IRR. Similarly, a property may appear to have a healthy yield, but when all factors are considered, it may turn out to have a comparatively low IRR. Thus, PIA can help you identify good investments, and just as importantly, help you avoid lemons.

Many people use PIA, including private investors, real estate agents, valuers, accountants, lawyers, and bank officers. Indeed, many of the people sending in their submissions for this book included PIA printouts to show just how good their investments are. One such printout was reproduced on page 47.

An entire chapter in the book *"Making Money in Residential Real Estate"* has been devoted to the Computer Analysis of Rates of Return. Furthermore, the appendix in the book *"Building Wealth in Changing Times"* describes and details the PIA software and how it may be used.

This software is available for either DOS, Windows 95/NT, or Macintosh platforms, at $595 + GST (see the order form on the last page).

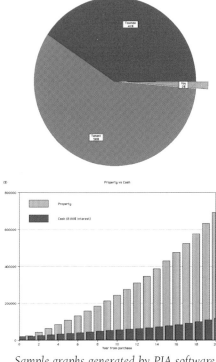

Sample graphs generated by PIA software

extraordinary profits

PROPERTY INVESTMENT ANALYSIS
software for property investors

PIA is a high performance computer program that provides an instant analysis of investment properties as an aid to acquisition decisions.

PIA calculates capital value, equity build-up, pre-tax cash flows, after tax returns, and the Internal Rate of Return (IRR) for up to 40 years ahead. Useful printouts enable investors to make wise investment decisions, while real estate agents can enhance and streamline their listings by including pertinent information for clients. Bank managers find the printouts invaluable in mortgage advance decision-making.

The program takes account of:
– depreciation (on both buildings and chattels)
– Solicitors' fees
– stamp duty (where applicable)
– mortgage interest payments
– mortgage structure (Interest Only or Principal plus Interest)
– loan application fees
– inflation rate
– capital growth rate
– investor's marginal tax rate
– negative gearing

Features:
– extremely simple to operate
– single screen full-colour spreadsheet layout
– full help facilities on screen, with prompts for input variables
– pre-selected values (defaults) for stamp duty rate, taxation rates, depreciation schedules, and loan acquisition fees
– instant sensitivity analysis to show effects of changes to any variable such as interest rates and rental levels
– prints two six-page reports including spreadsheets, tables and graphs
– calculates the tax benefits of an investment
– determines an investor's borrowing capacity
– DOS, Windows 95/NT and Mac versions available
– comes complete with a copy of the books *"The New Zealand Investor's Guide to Making Money in Residential Real Estate"*, *"Building Wealth through Investment Property"*, and *"Extraordinary Profits from Ordinary Properties"*.
– total cost is $595 plus GST

How to take advantage of other resources available to create wealth through real estate

With real estate, as with most other activities in life, you cannot hope to learn all you need to know by reading one book once. Although real estate is far more stable, consistent, and dependable than many other financial activities, keeping up with trends and ahead of the competition is imperative. Read many books on the subject (the book you don't read cannot help you!), attend seminars, talk with other investors, and dream up your own ideas to try out in the market place.

Success leaves clues! We have a number of resources to help both aspiring and seasoned investors. Please visit our web site www.dolfderoos.com to find out about our:

>   Books
>   Tape sets & CDs
>   Software/Videos
>   Mentoring program
>   Event schedule
>   New products, services and events

Finally, remember that contrary to the saying *knowledge is power*, it is only *applied* knowledge that is power. It is not enough to know a lot about real estate - to achieve real estate riches, you must put the theories into action. It's the difference between being interested and being committed.

Subscribe to our Free Monthly Newsletter

We trust that the resources available on our
Web site www.dolfderoos.com will empower you
and propel you on your way to not needing (or wanting)
a job thanks to real estate.